Original title:
Berries in the Breeze

Copyright © 2025 Creative Arts Management OÜ
All rights reserved.

Author: Lucas Harrington
ISBN HARDBACK: 978-1-80586-254-3
ISBN PAPERBACK: 978-1-80586-726-5

Sweetness Caught in a Breath

Tiny orbs in the air, oh what a sight,
They tickle our noses, a fruity delight.
With cherries that giggle and raspberries dance,
Each puff of the wind sparks a berry romance.

Fruits whisper secrets, as they tumble and roll,
Causing neighbors to chuckle, laughter takes hold.
The strawberries tease with a mischievous grin,
'Taste us,' they say, 'let the fun begin!'

The Color of Evening's Sigh

As sun dips low, cupped in a blush,
The bluebells chuckle, feeling the hush.
A swirl of tangerine, fuchsia, and gold,
Their hues tell a story, somewhat bold.

Grapes play tag with the shadows and light,
Tickled by twilight's jovial flight.
A berry parade, oh what a scene,
When laughter and twilight mix in between.

A Journey Through Ripening Hues

Rolling down hills, oh what a spree,
Mischief abounds, just you wait and see.
The blueberries chuckle in their sapphire suits,
While blackberries waltz with their leafy hoots.

On paths paved with sunshine, they skip and they slide,
Where raspberries tumble, there's no place to hide.
Each panting berry, from laughter so sweet,
Concocts a grand tale with each tiny tweet.

Laughter Among the Leaves

In the shade of a tree, gossip takes flight,
Leaves giggle softly, a whimsical sight.
With every soft rustle, a chuckle erupts,
Nature's own jester, nobody interrupts.

Dancing through branches, the wind joins the fun,
Tickling blossoms, 'Oh, sweet evening sun!'
Each leaf shares a joke, twisting in glee,
As fruits hold their bellies, how merry are we!

Nature's Kiss Under Starlit Skies

Tiny fruits bounce and sway,
A dance that's wild and gay.
Squirrels giggle, birds do cheer,
Harvest time is finally here!

Catch them quick, don't blink an eye,
They leap and twist, oh my, oh my!
With every pluck, a laugh is found,
As nature's giggle shakes the ground.

Harmonies of Rich Midnights

Underneath the glowing moon,
Fruits sing a crazy tune.
They bounce in clusters, what a sight,
A fruity band on a starry night!

Jelly jars are in a race,
With spreadable smiles in every place.
Laughter echoes down the lane,
As we squeeze the fruity gain.

Caresses of Sunlit Fields

Fields alive with sneaky charm,
Where fruits in sunlight cause alarm.
They wiggle out, they flirt, they play,
Add a pinch of fun to the day!

Pickers trip and tumble too,
While critters watch, saying boo!
Rolling laughter fills the air,
Harvest joy beyond compare!

Flavors of Freedom's Bounty

Taste the giggles on our tongues,
As tasty treats can't be outstrung.
Each little bite, a playful treat,
With silly sweetness, oh so neat!

Lemonade stands start to cheer,
As silly summer ends the year.
Fruits throw parties, smiles abound,
Every nook a joy is found!

Secrets of the Forest Floor

In the woods where critters hide,
Chasing snacks, the ants collide.
A squirrel slips, what a sight!
He drops his stash, oh what a plight!

Under leaves, the laughter streams,
As naughty gnomes craft their schemes.
Mushrooms giggle, dance in sun,
Nature's whimsy, all in fun!

A Symphony of Scarlet Delights

Crimson dots on leafy beds,
Tickle noses, bumping heads.
A plump one rolls with comical grace,
While rabbits race in the silly chase.

Jelly jars start to waltz,
With spoons that jive, oh what a fault!
Pip pip hooray, the jam does gleam,
Sweet on toast, it reigns supreme!

Nectar Cradled by Soft Sighs

Buzzing bees with dreamy eyes,
Whisper secrets, growling fries.
They sip the dew, so blissfully fat,
While lazy frogs just laugh and chat.

A dance of petals, round and round,
Fluttering smiles, no frowns are found.
Nectar dreams in sunlit gleam,
Nature's party, what a theme!

Serenade of the Ruby Harvest

A patch of red, what a sight,
Plump and juicy, oh what a bite!
Chipper birds with berry hats,
Chirp and chirp—imagine that!

Gather round, the feast is near,
As dandelions hold back a cheer.
Frolicsome squirrels join the fray,
Nibbling goodies through the day!

Gentle Secrets of Verdant Nights

In the garden, things do wiggle,
A berry snickers, gives a giggle.
The raccoons plot their cheeky heist,
While fireflies dance, they can't resist.

The moonlight casts a playful glow,
While frogs croak jokes, they steal the show.
A jester robin struts with flair,
Spreading laughter, everywhere!

Elixirs from Nature's Larder

A potion made from leaf and vine,
The raccon drinks, says, "Life's divine!"
The squirrels blend with daring zest,
Creating smoothies for a fest.

The ants parade in tiny hats,
While grasshoppers dance, wearing spats.
A brew of laughter fills the air,
As nature joins the silly fair!

Tones of Life's Vibrant Palette

Colors splatter on the path,
A playful splash, it makes me laugh.
The berries burst, a juicy mess,
A canvas where the critters guess.

A bluebird paints the sky with song,
While dandelions join along.
They giggle softly, what a sight,
As petals whirl in pure delight!

Sun-Soaked Elegance

Sunshine beams on velvet leaves,
A butterfly pirouettes, it weaves.
The ladybugs all cheer with glee,
In this dance of elegance, so free.

A lizard strikes a jazzy pose,
While bees hum sweetly as it goes.
Each creature wears a sunny grin,
In this warm glow, the fun begins!

Breeze-Borne Promises

Tiny globes dance in the air,
As squirrels plot with cheeky flair.
They whisper sweetly to the trees,
Insisting snacks are meant for me!

A gust of wind, and off they float,
In search of bliss, on nature's boat.
They giggle with each tiny drop,
Of juicy tales that just won't stop!

Chasing shadows under bright skies,
Pursuing mischief, they devise.
With laughter carried on a sigh,
Their little jests make grown-ups cry!

Heartbeats Among the Vines

In tangled vines, the laughter grows,
Where nature's jesters strike a pose.
With silly tricks, they tease the sun,
    Creating chaos, just for fun!

A plump rogue rolls with glee and flair,
As friends applaud from everywhere.
They dodge the bees with giggles loud,
As if they were the clowns, so proud!

Through laughter echoed, shadows prance,
With every bounce, a wobbly dance.
A merry chase through sunlight's charm,
These playful hearts mean no real harm!

The Language of Ripened Shores

On rolling waves, the giggles wave,
Their secrets spun, mischievous and brave.
With each tide's push, a cheeky smile,
The laughter rolls in curious style!

A tiny splash, a silly chat,
As sea gulls squawk and kids go splat!
With tossed sand castles all askew,
The shore's alive with jokes anew!

In every ripple, a story told,
Waves of laughter, purest gold.
These jolly whispers, bright and free,
Invite the world to join their spree!

Delicate Orbs on a Sunlit Path

Along the path, with giggles light,
The orbs drop hints in pure delight.
Inviting friends to join the chase,
In every plop, a smiling face!

A tumble here, a bounce-right-there,
They spark a chase without a care.
With bright hues trailing in their wake,
Adventure calls with every shake!

Laughter echoes, the sun is bright,
As every step feels just so right.
In this ballet of silly bliss,
Each fleeting moment brings a kiss!

Tides of Flavor in Midair

Up in the sky, a berry's game,
Bouncing on clouds, it calls your name.
With giggles and wiggles, they leap about,
A fruity tango, with laughs all out.

Watch them swirl through the warm sunshine,
Silly little snacks, so divine!
With a splash and a pop, they join the fun,
Turning summer days into a berry run.

Lush Secrets on Rustling Leaves

Hidden beneath where the whispers play,
Juicy delights have come out to play.
Tickled by winds, they chuckle with glee,
Hiding their sweetness, like little spree.

Leaves swagger like dancers, green and spry,
While twirling fruits wink from way up high.
Each rustle a laugh, each sigh a cheer,
Nature's own joke, could it be any clearer?

Nectar's Journey in the Air

Nectar clouds float with mischief and cheer,
Drifting along, they are so sincere.
Ticklehoney giggles as it swirls around,
In a bubble of laughter, joy does abound.

Buzzing along, they dance on the breeze,
Creating sweet giggles among the trees.
With each little drop, the world's in a spin,
Infusing the air, where the fun begins.

Petals and Shades of Blush

Petals parade in vibrant display,
While fruity faces come out to play.
With every blush under summer's gaze,
They chuckle aloud in their colorful ways.

A pink-dotted smile and an orange grin,
Cheery companions, the fun's about to begin.
Tickled by sunshine, they laugh in delight,
Join the merry dance, it's a colorful sight!

Glimmers of Forgotten Orchards

In the orchard, a squirrel prances,
Hiding snacks in his funny glances.
Apples giggle, they bounce and roll,
While pears tell secrets, that's their goal.

Robins dance in their feathery hats,
Chasing shadows, oh, imagine that!
A bee stumbles, quite out of tune,
Buzzing around like a quirky cartoon.

Jars of jam whisper tales so sweet,
Claiming victories in their fruity feat.
Strawberries wiggle, wanting to stand,
But they trip and fall, all unplanned.

Thus nature chuckles, a playful show,
Where laughter and colors freely flow.
Forget your worries, just let it be,
Join the fun, be wild, go free!

Magic Hidden in the Thicket

Underneath the leafy riddle,
A rabbit giggles, playing the fiddle.
Blackberries hide, bursting with cheer,
Messy little secrets, oh dear, oh dear!

A frog croaks jokes with a bulgy grin,
While fireflies twinkle, inviting you in.
Caterpillars dance in a conga line,
Waving their flags, "This party is mine!"

Nutty acorns gossip behind a tree,
"I told you so!" they shout with glee.
Hedgehogs tumble, all rolled in a heap,
Nature's own laughter is theirs to keep.

Come join the fun, the mischief, the banter,
In bushes of giggles, where pranks just can't slanter.
Each twist, each turn, an adventure to spurt,
In this hidden place, let joy be your shirt!

The Lightness of Vibrant Escapes

With a bounce and a skip, they dash through the field,
Where dandelions laugh, their secrets revealed.
Bursts of color, wild and bright,
A joyful canvas, pure delight.

A plump little mouse throws a berry spree,
As butterflies giggle around in glee.
The sun peeks in, casting silly shadows,
While raccoons practice their best muddy meadows.

Frolicsome winds play tag with the trees,
Rustling leaves with the utmost ease.
A curious snail, with its shell all around,
Hitches a ride on the fun without sound.

Watch the mushrooms shake hands with the sun,
They form a club for everyone fun.
So dance like the flowers, sing like the breeze,
Ah, let's party beneath the green leaves!

Enchanted by Nature's Abundance

In a patch of laughter, the sunshine glows,
Sweet surprises peek, where nobody knows.
Jelly beans tumble from an overhead cloud,
While giggling mushrooms gather a crowd.

The joyful bumblebee, with a quirky hum,
Bounds from petal to petal, what fun!
While thickets engage in a game of hide,
And each little critter is filled with pride.

Juicy delights drip from the skies,
Pouring sweetness, oh how time flies!
Daring dew drops, they catch on a thorn,
Then burst into laughter at the crack of dawn.

So here in this wonder, so silly and bright,
Each moment with nature feels just right.
Join the jubilation, let your heart sway,
In this magical place, come laugh and play!

Wandering Through Fields of Abundance

In the fields where laughter grows,
I tripped on something, who knows?
A raspberry rolled, a frisky friend,
I chased it down, oh, what a blend!

Sunshine giggled, tickling the vine,
A grape jumped up, 'Hey, this is fine!'
I slipped and slid, like in a dance,
Fruits plotting fun, all in a prance!

With every stumble, a fruit parade,
Mangoes chuckled, lemons dismayed.
I laughed so hard, I shed a tear,
The fruits conspired, "Let's keep him here!"

Oh, fields of joy where silly meets sweet,
Each juicy laugh, a tasty treat!
I wandered on, lost in delight,
In the land of laughter, everything's bright!

The Promise of Juicy Wonderland

In a land where splashes reign,
Fruits flirt while I complain.
"Hey there, peach, don't roll away!"
"Catch me if you can!" it says with sway.

Clouds above burst into cheer,
Kiwis doing backflips, oh dear!
A melon winks, quite out of range,
"Join our party, it's time for a change!"

I stumbled into a blueberry patch,
One winked at me—what a catch!
I laughed aloud, "What's in your tea?"
"Just a splash of zest, come taste with glee!"

In this zany sweet delight,
Every fruit just feels so right.
With a giggle and gulp, I'd swear,
Juicy Wonderland is beyond compare!

A Serenade Amidst the Vines

Underneath the shade of green,
Fruits rehearsing for a scene.
"Strawberries, act cool!" one cried,
As they jived, my stomach sighed.

Vines began a waltz, so grand,
"Wanna join?" it made a band!
With every note and fruity cheer,
I felt a giggle drawing near.

Cherries winked with cheeky grace,
Raspberries rolled in a playful race.
"Don't let the humans steal the show!"
I joined the dance, giving it a go!

With a twirl and a burst of zest,
Fruits inspired my very best.
In their world of humor and rhyme,
A serenade that defies all time!

Whispers of Fruit-Laden Vines

In the garden, laughter spills,
Chuckles rise among the hills.
Chubby cheeks and stained shirts,
Giggling while picking dessert blirts.

Wobbly vines twist in a dance,
Fruit hangs low, they take a chance.
Swinging low, they tease the bees,
Honey drips with silly wheezes.

A rascally squirrel plots with glee,
Thinking he can outsmart me.
I toss a berry, he does a flip,
But I'm fast, I just won this trip.

The juiciest prize, halved and shared,
Also stains the dog, unprepared.
We laugh so hard, it's pure delight,
Summer's joy is a wild flight.

Dance of the Summer Juices

Underneath the summer sky,
Juices flow while giggles fly.
Each squished fruit, a sticky mess,
Making juice in nature's dress.

We dance 'round with silly flair,
Splashing juice everywhere.
With leaps and bounds, we hit the ground,
A fruity shower all around.

The blender rocks with blinding speed,
While mustard-colored ants take heed.
A popsicle prank, we can't resist,
It melts too fast, oh how they twist!

In a bowl, a mess of red,
Friends could laugh until they're dead.
For every sip, there comes a laugh,
Nature's drink brings happy craft.

Sweetness on the Wind

A breeze whispers, what a tease,
Fruit aromas dance with ease.
Penguins in sunglasses stroll, oh dear,
Even the worms come out to cheer!

Pies and tarts rule the fair,
While raccoons gobble without a care.
Each licked finger tells a story,
Of sweet mishaps and fruit-fueled glory.

Mom's dessert, a curious sight,
Caught in the curtains, what a fright!
Giggles burst as the cat leaps in,
With frosting paws, let the fun begin!

A juice fight here, a splash over there,
Squeals and crumbs fill the air.
We gather round, a juicy blend,
This fruity joy never seems to end.

Scarlet Dreams in Sunlight

In the sun, a splash of red,
Mischief brewing, that's what's said.
We crown the king of silly snacks,
With fruity robes and berry hacks.

A race to gather, who will win?
Berry kings or berry kin?
Stains of laughter mark the ground,
Chasing dreams where joy is found.

With jelly hands, we throw a cheer,
Muffin tops will disappear.
Sipping nectar from a yellow cup,
Each tiny sip, we simply erupt!

And as dusk paints skies all around,
Contented sighs are the only sound.
We're left with stains and dreams that gleam,
In a summertime, juicy dream.

The Tranquility of Hidden Gardens

In gardens where the whispers play,
Tiny wonders dance and sway.
Red and blue, a sweet parade,
Chasing shadows that won't fade.

A squirrel sneaks a berry snack,
With his friends, they urge him back.
Laughter fills the leafy space,
As ants attempt a silly race.

Petals tickle toes that trip,
Spilling nectar with each slip.
Nature's jokes, oh so absurd,
Tickling souls, not a word heard.

In this joy, we lose all sense,
Of why we came—was it the fence?
In every blush and every hue,
Life's a giggle, fresh and new.

Starlight's Embrace on Earthly Delights

Under starlight, giggles soar,
Frolicking feet on the forest floor.
Plump little wonders peek and grin,
While crickets play their violin.

Moonlit paths of mischief gleam,
Where frogs and fireflies love to dream.
The fruits of night, they take a bow,
"Who knew we'd be the stars now?"

Bouncing branches, oh what fun!
Silly raccoons race and run.
In this revelry, we can't resist,
Trying not to get too blissed.

So come, let's dance, let laughter ring,
Join the chorus, let's all sing.
Under starlit skies so bright,
We find joy, instant delight.

Breezes Carrying Forgotten Flavors

Whispers drift on zephyr wings,
Reminding us of funny things.
A gust of wind, a taste surprise,
As giggles catch, and laughter flies.

An old pie left behind the bush,
Turns lunchtime into a funny hush.
The taste of laughter, pure delight,
Savory treats in the night light.

Round red cheeks and muddled glee,
Chasing flavors, wild and free.
Fruits that tumble into our hands,
Leave us grinning as life expands.

So take a bite of whimsy's fare,
Savor sweetness, toss your care.
With breezes wild, we'll share the bliss,
Of hidden flavors, we won't miss.

Drawn to Earthly Whimsy

In meadows green where laughter grows,
The secrets hide in newfound prose.
Bouncing bubbles, jeweled treats,
Whimsy dances on tiny feet.

A hedgehog dons a berry hat,
Looks so dapper—imagine that!
He grins at us with such delight,
As he flees into the night.

Wobbling worms in silly lines,
Plotting tiny wild designs.
Grasshoppers join the conga line,
Where whimsy rules and all's divine.

Each twist and turn, a playful tease,
Life spins round in jokes with ease.
So raise a cheer for every whim,
In this dance, let's not be dim!

Fragrant Embrace of Wildness

In the field where mischief thrives,
Little fruits play hide and seek,
Tickling noses, laughing jives,
Every bite's a burst, so cheeky!

A smiling sun shines overhead,
Poking fun at clouds so gray,
"Don't go home!" the wild things said,
"Stay and dance, come what may!"

With hands all sticky, hearts so free,
We giggle as we race with glee,
Grapes roll by like tiny cars,
We'll paint the world in fruit-shaped stars!

Lemonade giggles, raspberry screams,
Nature's jokers, bursting seams,
Laughter ripples, flavors mix,
Join the fun—let's share the fix!

Rainbow Hues in Lively Currents

Twists and turns of color bold,
Strawberry hats on heads of green,
Playful laughter, stories told,
Joyful misfits on the scene.

Blueberries bouncing, such a sight,
Dancing round like little mice,
Swirling, twirling, what a night!
In this madcap, fruity spice.

Banana slips and berry spills,
Echoes of our gleeful shrieks,
Nature's playground, endless thrills,
A canvas painted with our peaks!

With flavors as our guiding muse,
We savor each zany aim,
Creating chaos we can't refuse,
Laughter echoing our claim!

Nature's Edible Artistry

A canvas spread beneath the sky,
Colors splatter, flavors blend,
Nature's feast, oh my, oh my!
Taste bud artists, let's transcend!

Pineapple shouts, "Try me for fun!"
While figs and pears do comic dances,
In this playground, joy has won—
Where even grapes wear silly pantses!

Playful jitters, sweet debates,
"Who's the juiciest?" we declare,
Between the giggles, nature waits,
For our laughter to fill the air!

Crunch and munch, we sing our tune,
Each bite a boisterous ballet,
Nature's stage, the sun a moon,
Edible art in bright array!

The Agile Choreography of Taste

In the garden, what a treat,
Fruity dancers, swift and spry,
Raspberry leaps with nimble feet,
While lemon twirls up to the sky!

A tango fresh on dewy grass,
Blueberries pop in playful skits,
Nature's groove, no time to pass,
We join the fun, a zestful blitz!

Juicy pirouettes, sweet all-around,
With every munch, the laughter swells,
Strawberry jumps and then rebounds,
In this circus, taste befells!

Banana splits, our tag team shouts,
Sips of sweetness, giggly yowls,
Each flavor gleefully flouts,
A merry dance that bobs and prowls!

A Garden's Whisper Among the Senses

In the garden, laughter grows,
Tickling petals, tickling toes,
Bees are buzzing, oh what fun,
Shaking leaves in the bright sun.

Red and round, they wiggle free,
Rolling down to tease a bee,
Fragrant scents that make you grin,
Who knew fruits could wear such skin?

Chasing shadows, playing hide,
With a berry tucked inside,
Nature's mischief, oh so bright,
Wonders sprout from morning's light.

Giggling plants hold secrets tight,
Under the moon, they dance at night,
Whispers echo, teasing fate,
In this orchard, life is great!

Dreams Wrapped in Lush Colors

Colors twirl in sweet delight,
Carts all filled and spirits bright,
Blue and red, a rolling cheer,
Fruits call out, 'Come pick us here!'

Jesters dress in leafy gowns,
Swirling laughter all around,
In the orchard, joy's a feast,
Nature's party—never ceased.

Squishy bites and juicy thrills,
Every taste brings hearty spills,
As I dance through sunlit rows,
A fruit parade just overflows.

Whirls of flavor make me sway,
Cheeky smiles on this bright day,
Nature's paintbrush strokes so bold,
Wraps my heart in colors told.

Flavors Embraced by Time

Juicy laughter fills the air,
Time slows down, without a care,
Sugary bursts all intertwined,
Snacks that make the heart feel fined.

A wobble here, a giggle there,
Fruit conquests beyond compare,
Chasing sweetness down the lane,
Savoring joy, free from pain.

What's that bouncing past my head?
Strawberries, maybe jam instead?
A fruity wind, now here it comes,
Tickling my nose, oh here it hums!

Memories swirl on summer's breath,
With every nibble, tempt the depth,
In this feast, let's play the mime,
For in each munch, we grasp at time.

Charmed Currents of Nature's Blood

Nature's pulse begins to thrum,
Fruits like drummers, here they come,
Performing tunes on the green stage,
A vibrant show; life's all the rage.

Charmed by sunlight, cheeky spree,
Dancing lightly, wild and free,
Swapping stories on the vine,
All agree, it's tasting time!

A berry jumps, oh watch it fly,
Chasing dreams beneath the sky,
With every bounce, the giggles grow,
As each fruit steals quite the show!

In this carnival of delight,
Joy is wrapped in morning light,
With every chuckle, taste, and tease,
Life's a joke beneath the trees!

The Orchard's Gentle Lullaby

In the orchard, the fruits do sway,
Twisting, turning, in a playful display.
A squirrel in a hat sings a tune,
While the sun giggles, it's afternoon!

A hedgehog dances with a nearby vine,
Wobbling along, it thinks it's divine.
Chirping birds join in on the fun,
Joking about who will be number one!

The apples debate their hue and size,
While plump cherries exchange cheeky lies.
"Who's juicier?" they laugh and gloat,
As the wind whispers, "You're all afloat!"

So we stroll through rows of merry treats,
Where laughter echoes, and joy repeats.
In this orchard of folly, we play our part,
Taking a slice of nature's art!

Ripe Delights on a Breezy Afternoon

Under the shade, the laughter rolls,
Pies are baking, filling our souls.
A plum winks, oh so bold,
While strawberries tease, their tales unfold.

"Who's the sweetest?" a ripe peach shouts,
To everyone's giggles and silly doubts.
Oh, the mischief that gentle wind brings,
As fruits twirl about on invisible strings!

A raspberry dons glasses, looking quite sly,
Sipping on juice, waving goodbye.
"Come and taste!" it shouts with glee,
While blueberries join in a shout: "Yippee!"

Here's to the laughter upon the green,
To juicy delights that dance unseen.
With each grin, and each hearty cheer,
We celebrate the harvest, year after year!

A Symphony of Nature's Harvest

In fields of verdant, wild delight,
The fruits engage in a mock debate fight.
A grape leaps high, quite full of cheer,
"Who will be eaten first?" it sneers!

Cucumbers giggle in leafy beds,
While chatting cucumbers swap funny threads.
"Let's race to the basket, let's make it a game!
The winner gets eaten, oh what a fame!"

Ripe bananas throw a party so loud,
Inviting all fruits from the nearby crowd.
Peaches tango with nectarines in sight,
Spinning around till it feels just right.

Their laughter rings out, a joyous tune,
Beneath a warm, chuckling afternoon moon.
This harvest isn't just a treat,
It's laughter and fun, oh so sweet!

Sun-Kissed Orbs of Joy

On a sunny day, fruits bounce with pride,
One little berry attempts to hide.
"Catch me if you can!" it shouts with glee,
Spinning like a top, oh what a spree!

Ripe mangoes plot their fruity schemes,
While pumpkins giggle in sunlit dreams.
"Who has the best shade?" the melons ask,
Daring each other in this juicy task.

Cherished moments in nature's bright light,
With cherries and figs, oh what a sight!
The laughter rings as they play their part,
Sun-kissed orbs, the joy in our heart!

So we gather 'round, with smiles so wide,
To savor the fun, let nothing subside.
With every nibble and song we sing,
In this fruity panorama, happiness springs!

Nature's Colorful Whispers

In the garden, giggles rise,
As raspberries roll like little spies.
Blueberries tumble, what a spree,
They bounce around, wild and free.

Cherries try to wear a crown,
Splattering juice all over town.
With every twist, a fruit parade,
A riot of color in sun and shade.

Laughing leaves join in the fun,
Dancing shadows under the sun.
The strawberries tease with their sweet notes,
While ants march on in tiny coats.

Nature whispers tales so bright,
Where every fruit is pure delight.
In this carnival of tastes and cheer,
Every nibble comes with a cheer!

Harvesting Hues of Twilight

Under the dusk, a flavor fight,
Purple and red in fading light.
Peaches prance and plums do jig,
While lemons play the dance of fig.

I spotted a rogue, a cantaloupe,
Swinging high on a berry's hope.
Watermelons rolling on the ground,
In this twilight, joy is found.

Squash joins in with a cheeky grin,
As beetroot glows from deep within.
Raspberry whispers, 'Unleash the fun!'
As fruit escapades have just begun.

Twilight's hues, a fruity prize,
The shiniest fruits in such a size.
With laughter mixed in evening's blend,
The harvest here will never end!

Embrace of the Summer Veil

Summer rolls in with a fluffy hat,
While fruits conspire, imagine that!
Fuzzy peaches are plotting pranks,
As they hide behind green leafy ranks.

Maraschino cherries in a line,
Try to sneak some sunshine wine.
Blackberries boast of their dark charm,
While orange slices cause alarm.

Melons sing with a juicy giggle,
As kids come near, and they all wiggle.
The raspberry leaves wave and tease,
Inviting laughter on the breeze.

Draped in colors, summer's art,
A tapestry of joy to impart.
In this embrace, sweet and wily,
Every fruit dances, oh so silly!

The Allure of Forgotten Pastures

In fields once lush, a party waits,
With nature's snacks on serving plates.
Daisies giggle, come join the fray,
As forgotten fruits come out to play.

Crisp currents whisper a playful tune,
While wild grapes swing beneath the moon.
The elderberries chuckle and sway,
Inviting all to join their ballet.

Under the stars, a harvest feast,
With every nibble, laughter's released.
Nutty dandelions let out a cheer,
As fruit forks dance, drawing near.

Pastures hold secrets, bright and spry,
Where flavors mingle and spirits fly.
In this allure, joy does not fade,
As nature's bounty becomes a parade!

The Sweetness of Evening Air

In the garden, chuckles grow,
Where laughter dances with the flow.
The fruit hangs low, in cheeky glee,
Whispers joke, "Come pick me!"

Squirrels prance, their tails in flight,
Swapping tales of sweet delight.
They taste a snack, then run away,
Sharing giggles at the play.

Ripe and jolly, colors clash,
Rolling round in a happy dash.
A plump delight, so bold and round,
Fetch a fork, and munch the ground!

Under the stars, a giggle heard,
As nature hums its quirky bird.
With each bite, a silly grin,
Oh, the joy of fruity spin!

A Dance of Nature's Gems

Swinging low, the juicy crew,
In their hats of green and dew.
They shimmy, twist, and break the silence,
Mocking nature's sweet defiance.

Bees are buzzing, oh what fun,
Twirling 'round like a carousel spun.
They wear their shades, so cool and sly,
While butterflies join in the sky.

Jigging fruits, all ripe and bright,
Swinging to the moon's soft light.
Giggling trees sway in the song,
A fruity dance, we all belong.

As the night starts to unfold,
These sparkling gems are brave and bold.
With every nibble, joy takes flight,
Nature's party feels just right!

Fragrance of Summer's Lullaby

The air is sweet, a silly tune,
With scents of sunshine, afternoon.
Folks are dancing, all in jest,
Hilarity pops from berry's nest.

Sipping joy from cups of cheer,
With every laugh, the world feels near.
A splash of color joins the cheer,
As nature frets, "You'll make me veer!"

Jelly jars are wobbling tight,
Dancing snacks parade the night.
Chubby cheeks with joy abound,
As fruity giggles swirl around.

With every breeze, there's a chime,
Nature chuckles, feeling prime.
So raise your glass to merry air,
In this world, no room for care!

Crimson Kisses on Gentle Winds

Tickled by the playful breeze,
Mocks the fruits, as they aim to please.
Swaying low with every spin,
Silly laughter, let's begin!

The sun winks with a golden grin,
As nature plays a joyous hymn.
Rolling fruits tumble and shout,
Join the fun—there's joy throughout!

Hummingbirds dip and swirl,
They play tag with a swirly twirl.
Laughter bursts, colors bright,
A fruity feast, oh what a sight!

In this garden of delight,
Silliness takes its joyful flight.
Crimson kisses chase the day,
As giggles lead the silly way!

Radiance of a Glowing Meadow

In fields where laughter grows tall,
Little fruits make a merry call.
With giggles hiding in the sun,
They wink at birds, a cheeky fun.

The insects dance in silly trails,
While gophers wear their tiny veils.
A rabbit hops with a jolly stride,
And each swirl brings another ride.

Butterflies play tag on the breeze,
While squirrels debate their favorite cheese.
Nature's circus with a twist,
Not a moment that you could miss.

So raise a glass of fruity cheer,
To berry jokes we hold so dear.
In meadows bright, where joy won't cease,
The world sings out with wild release.

Echoes of Autumn's Promise

When leaves drop like confetti mad,
The ground is dressed in orange glad.
Giggling seeds all start to roll,
While pumpkins plot to take control.

A quirky crow steals acorn hats,
While hedgehogs zoom on little mats.
The apple tree plays hide and seek,
As winds blow whispers, mild yet cheeky.

Squirrels stash snacks with dramatic flair,
While rabbits snooze without a care.
The harvest moon shines, bold and bright,
Casting pranks on a chilly night.

So as we munch on cider treats,
In laughter, every autumn meets.
The echoes ring, a joyful tune,
As nature sways beneath the moon.

Lush Treasures of the Earth

In gardens rich with colors bright,
The veggies plot a sneaky fight.
Radishes wear coats of green,
As carrots plan their next routine.

Pineapple spins with dapper style,
While lettuce grins, a leafy smile.
The radish struts on tiny feet,
With each new dance, they can't be beat.

The herbs all giggle, sharing tea,
While beetroot blushes, cannot flee.
As cucumbers crack up at the scene,
And peas pop out to intervene.

So join the party, don't be late,
With every taste, it's simply great.
A feast of joy, each bite a laugh,
In gardens where we find our path.

Tasting the Lightness of Air

When summer swirls on a playful whim,
The breeze carries fruit, oh so dim.
A cloud of joy floats in the sky,
While laughter's scent can never die.

The melon sings a soft, sweet tune,
While cherries argue who's the moon.
Each little berry wears a grin,
Inviting all to jump right in.

With picnic baskets packed tight,
The ants all dance in sheer delight.
While lemonade's a fizzy cheer,
Nature's laugh is loud and clear.

So sip the air and munch away,
On nature's gifts this sunny day.
A world so light, so full of fun,
Where every moment's a tasty run.

The Sweet Dance of Nature's Palette

In a garden full of glee,
Colors twirl with wild spree.
Blue buns hop, and red ones roll,
Dancing sweetly, heart and soul.

Laughter spills with every sway,
Nature's paintbrush in the play.
Yellow giggles, purple cheer,
Who knew fruits could be so dear?

The sun takes part, a shining grin,
As they bounce and spin within.
With a wink, the breeze declares,
A fruity circus takes the airs!

So come join this fruity fest,
Taste the joy, it's truly best.
With each pluck and every bite,
Nature's palette, pure delight!

Juicy Tales from the Thicket

In the thicket where we roam,
Fruits are chatting, feeling home.
A raspberry spills a juicy yarn,
While blackberries clone a barn.

A strawberry tells a silly tale,
Of how it once met a gale.
With a laugh, the elder folk,
Join in on this fruity joke.

A cherry swoops in with style,
Claims it can run a whole mile.
Then slips on a dew-drenched leaf,
And bounces back, beyond belief!

Giggles echo, jokes unfold,
In this thicket, stories told.
With each laugh, the shadows bloom,
Juicy tales break the gloom!

Nature's Lullaby in Shades of Red

Beneath the trees, where leaves do sway,
Crimson dreams frolic and play.
A plump fruit winks with delight,
Singing softly through the night.

"Hey there, friend, don't you be shy,
Join our red parade, oh my!"
A cherry's jig brings forth a grin,
As acorns tap and crickets spin.

With each whisper of the breeze,
Nature hums and sways with ease.
A raspy tune from near a vine,
Of summer fun and sun divine!

So lay back, let laughter flow,
In shades of red, the joy will grow.
A lullaby of sweet reprise,
As stars waltz through velvet skies.

A Tidal Wave of Colorful Tenderness

Waves of color crash about,
Fruits in laughter, none in doubt.
A splash of red, a dash of blue,
Tickling toes, a fruity hue.

Pineapples slide in slick delight,
Tangerines giggle all through the night.
"Best stay afloat," one lime yells loud,
But it tumbles down, a silent crowd!

Plums wave flags like royalty,
At this fruity jubilee.
Berries blow kisses on the shore,
Inviting all for a snack galore!

So here's to waves of fruity fun,
Underneath the shining sun.
Join the mix, let colors fuse,
In this tenderness, let's all cruise!

A Tapestry of Lush Delights

A round, red fruit on a sunny trail,
Teases the raccoon with a fruity tale.
Chasing delight, it slips on a peel,
Lands in a patch—a berry's big deal.

Ants host a party, they dance on the ground,
Swinging their legs, making funny sounds.
With a splash of juice, they start to play,
Creating a trend on this fruit buffet.

Squirrels wear hats made of leafy greens,
Throwing a feast like kings and queens.
Mice take a selfie, their smiles so wide,
As the bright little fruits roll down the slide.

Up in the trees, a dispute takes flight,
Who gets the last chunk of pure delight?
While all the chatter creates quite a fuss,
The berries just giggle, 'It's all made for us!'

Vibrant Notes in the Air

A plump little treasure swings from a vine,
Whistling a melody—oh, how divine!
Birds join the chorus, with beaks full of cheer,
Even the worms hum a tune we can hear.

The sun winks at clouds, tossing fruit into play,
Like confetti flung high on a merry day.
Balloons made of laughter float up with glee,
As the wind carries tunes of fruit folly.

In a patchy dance-off, a beetle takes flight,
Spinning around like it's Friday night.
With every twist, more berries join in,
Like a fruity parade where all are akin.

The breeze plays a prank, tickling the leaves,
While chatterbugs share the stories with thieves.
What happens next is anyone's guess,
When nature erupts in pure fruitiness!

Shadows of Midnight's Favors

Under the glow of a moonlit prank,
Creatures assemble near the berry bank.
With giggles and whispers, they gather 'round,
For a midnight feast, sweet joy is found.

A cheeky raccoon, wearing shades of night,
Tries to juggle fruits—it's a slippery sight!
With each little tumble, laughter does bloom,
As berries roll out, lighting the gloom.

Foxes wear capes and take to the sky,
Holding berry crowns, oh, look at them fly!
They swoosh and they soar, causing such glee,
In this fruity ballet, all wild and free.

The saga unfolds, with a twist and a shout,
Who spilt the juice? Oh, did you see that sprout?
As shadows sway, under twinkling stars,
It's a berry bash that echoes from Mars!

The Taste of Wandering Spirits

Flavors collide in the misty night air,
Haunted by laughter, they dance with a flair.
Whimsical whispers tease the lost souls,
While fruit floats by on its own little strolls.

Goblins sip nectar, singing sweet tunes,
While pixies throw sprinkles that shine like the moons.
They twirl with delight, a wild, fruity mess,
With shadows engaged in a playful game of chess.

A ghostly banana slips and does glide,
Across a patch where the lost spirits hide.
They chuckle and howl, in vibrant delight,
At this nightly feast, what a glorious sight!

In this whimsical world where flavors ignite,
Each twist brings laughter, a true joyous fright.
As the night slips away, memories please,
Captured by echoes of joy in the breeze.

Coastal Fruition of Imagination

On a picnic shore, a thought arose,
Dancing fruits in hats, they struck a pose.
Seagulls tried to steal, what a silly sight,
But the peaches rolled fast, oh what a flight!

Jelly beans were surfing, on a jelly wave,
While licorice seaweed danced, all brave.
Lemonade waves splashed with zest,
Nature's party, a fruity fest!

Grapes played tag with the wandering breeze,
Under candy clouds, they scurried with ease.
Each berry laughed and spun around,
While giggling flowers twirled on the ground.

With sunshine giggling, what a delight,
Every sweet treat brought pure delight.
Imagine the fun, a coastal spree,
Where laughter and joy fill the sea!

The Playful Caress of Nature's Confection

In the garden's arms, a twist of fate,
Strawberries decide to dance with a plate.
Marshmallow vines stretched high and wide,
With gummy worms twirling, side by side!

A cupcake's balloon floated up above,
Whispering sweet nothings, the bees fell in love.
Raspberry giggles echoed through the plot,
As cherries debated who's the sweetest lot.

Blueberries juggled, oh what a mess,
Doughnuts rolled in, demanding finesse.
Together they formed a wild parade,
Nature's circus, so cleverly made!

Pineapple hats on the heads of the crew,
While peaches donned shades, looking brand new.
The laughter erupted, nature's delight,
In this sugary world, everything's bright!

Whispers of Wild Harvest

The garden held secrets, green and round,
While mischievous carrots danced on the ground.
Tomatoes were gossiping, red in their blush,
As cucumbers giggled in a leafy hush.

Pumpkins donned glasses, presenting a show,
With peas in their pods, all ready to go.
A berry brigade marched, a rowdy troop,
Jellybeans joined in, creating a loop.

Radishes rolled into a comical spin,
As onions shed tears for a laughter win.
Each herb chimed in with a fragrant cheer,
While the sun winked down, bringing warmth near.

Harvest whispers floated, in breezy delight,
Nature's laughter echoed, day turned to night.
The playful charm of this harvest fair,
Left smiles on faces and joy in the air!

Dappled Sunlight on Juicy Dreams

In the orchard's bright glow, a zany scene,
Fruits donned costumes, looking quite keen.
With cherries in capes and pears in a twist,
They planned a parade, oh what a fist!

Citrus were juggling, lemons and limes,
While dragonfruit rapped in melodic rhymes.
The laughter erupted, as colors collided,
Nature's own festival, so joyfully provided.

Peaches in polka dots, dancing all day,
While watermelons lined up in a ballet.
Raspberries tumbled, in a playful mess,
With every sweet giggle, they aimed to impress.

The sunlight streamed down, dappling bright,
Each fruity character basked in delight.
In whimsical harmony, dreams did arise,
A fruity escapade beneath sunny skies!

Harvesting Memory in Soft Zephyrs

In the garden, a giggle grows,
Under the leaves, a secret shows.
Bouncing berries in a playful strife,
Pocketfuls of laughter, oh what a life!

The wind whispers tales, both silly and sweet,
Of plump little fruits, a whimsical treat.
They roll and they tumble, up high and down low,
With each little bounce, more giggles do flow!

Old memories swirl with the fragrant air,
As critters join in, causing a rare scare.
A squirrel in a hat, a rabbit with style,
Dancing through orchards with grand little smiles!

So here in this haven, with joy we will dwell,
Harvest time stories, oh how they swell.
With each twist and turn, our hearts take to flight,
In the soft zephyrs, laughter ignites!

Laughter and Flavor in the Garden's Heart

A dance of delight in the sunbeam's glow,
Fruits tickle the tongue, where sweet rivers flow.
Berry stains on cheeks, a mischievous sight,
As giggles erupt in the warm afternoon light.

The bees hum a tune that's vibrant and bold,
While ants wear their crowns made of marigold.
A game of hopscotch on clumps of green grass,
Each hop sends a berry rolling right past!

In the midst of the fun, a koala dropped by,
Sipping nectar from blossoms, oh my oh my!
His dance is delightful, his moves a surprise,
With each little twirl, you can't help but rise!

Together we savor both humor and taste,
No time for regrets or measures of haste.
In laughter we forge the flavors we crave,
In the garden's heart, let memories save!

Echoes of the Verdant Canopy

In shadows that giggle among the tall trees,
Loud whispers of fun float along with the breeze.
A chatter of critters, all up in a fuss,
While munching on snacks, there's just no rush!

With colors all splattered like paint on a wall,
Laughter erupts with each stumbling fall.
A cheeky raccoon with a berry-filled pouch,
Steals the show from a scraggly old grouch!

As vines twist and twirl, they playfully tease,
While sunbeams flicker like dance partners, please.
Silly old shadows, as creatures do roam,
Creating a symphony, this wild woodland home!

Echoes of joy through each leafy lane,
In the laughter of nature, no room for plain.
The canopy sways with secrets to share,
In the verdant, we find funny moments laid bare!

The Tantalizing Dance of Color

A burst of the rainbow, where fruits laugh and play,
In the morning light, they greet the new day.
Blue and red giggles, a zesty ballet,
While green sprites twirl in a jazzy display!

The flavor parade, such a fresh, funny show,
As plump little spheres chase the wind to and fro.
"Catch me if you can!" they confidently cheek,
While butterflies chuckle, hiding their peek!

In this fest of delight, we partake with glee,
A feast for the senses, just you and me.
With splashes of sunshine, that's how we sway,
As we munch on the joy that won't ever decay!

So here's to the colors, the laughter, the light,
Dancing through gardens, all pure delight.
In the tapestry woven by nature's embrace,
Funny little moments take us to a new place!

Rustling Secrets in the Canopy

In the trees, a chatter flies,
Little critters share their spies,
Whispering secrets, oh so sweet,
Dodging lunch, a fruity treat.

Squirrels jump with berries bold,
Nibbles here, a stash of gold,
A raccoon laughs, it's quite the show,
Stealing snacks, then back to tow.

In the thicket, they convene,
Jelly stains on paws pristine,
Rolling laughter through the glade,
As fruit-filled antics soon invade.

With each rustle, giggles rise,
Nature's pranks beneath the skies,
A fruity world where all concoct,
Sweet mischief, they can't be stopped.

Bursting with Nature's Secrets

Red and blue in shadows hide,
Nature's treasure, wild and wide,
Jumps of joy from every vine,
A gobble here, a silly line.

The fox, it prances, with a grin,
Chasing tales of fruity spin,
In the chaos, laughter grows,
Splattered juice on little toes.

Sunshine spills on fluffy tails,
As giggles dance in gentle gales,
In the patch, a playful race,
Nature's jest, a berry chase.

Every nibble, a comical tale,
Silly dances start to prevail,
As laughter bursts, sweet and bright,
Nature's joy in full delight.

Dreamscape of Lush Flavors

In a garden of dreams divine,
Colors pop, all align,
Fruits of laughter, bold and round,
Where playful spirits leap and bound.

A strawberry tickles a cheek,
A raspberry whispers, 'Hey, let's sneak!'
Eggplants giggle, a purple glee,
In this patch, they're wild and free.

Mirthful vines curl and twist,
In this world, none could resist,
Each pluck brings a giggle spree,
In this lush absurdity.

Under a sky so vibrant and blue,
Fruity laughter swells anew,
A comical feast where all can thrive,
In this dreamscape, we come alive.

A Canvas of Fruity Sunbeams

On a canvas of sunlit cheer,
Colors splash from far and near,
Watermelon giggles with delight,
While oranges join the fruit-filled flight.

Mango dances in the rays,
Swinging hips and sunny plays,
Peaches tumble, oh what a sight,
Rolling down in pure delight.

A fruit bouquet starts to sing,
Jubilant joy in every spring,
As cherries toss a playful jest,
A canvas painted with zest and fest.

In this art of flavors bold,
Funny tales of sweetness told,
Where every drop of playful sun,
Creates a feast, laughter spun.

Fruitful Whimsy in the Wind

Tiny fruits dance and sway,
Their laughter brightens the day.
They tease the squirrels with a grin,
While birds all gather round, to spin.

A cherry winks from leafy shade,
That sneaky smile; could it be played?
The raspberries giggle in delight,
As they bounce around, taking flight.

The tartness calls with a playful pounce,
As bumblebees spin and bounce.
Each little snack a joke in bloom,
Spreading giggles in the afternoon.

So grab your hat, and join the fun,
Join in the games, don't be outdone.
For in this patch of fruity cheer,
Every laugh brings summer near!

A Feast for the Senses

Sour and sweet collide in a swirl,
The color parade begins to unfurl.
A blueberry bows, oh so shy,
While honeysuckle sips the sky.

A strawberry flirts with a plump peach,
Tasting their joy, can you reach?
In this feast of juicy delight,
Each bite is a giggle, pure and bright.

Bouncing currants race with glee,
While little ants climb the tree.
A picnic sprawls, so silly and nice,
As fruit takes turns in this slice of life.

So gather 'round with a grin so wide,
Join the dance, let the fun be your guide.
For each little nibble, each playful tease,
Brings joy that floats upon the breeze!

Hidden Gems in Nature's Palette

In patches bright, they hide away,
Little jewels come out to play.
With a wink and a jolly cheer,
They tempt all critters far and near.

A raspberry hat with a cheeky flair,
Mocks the carrots who start to stare.
While wise old apples sit with ease,
Offering wisdom, as they tease.

Blackberries wrestling in a row,
Sticky sweet chaos; what a show!
Each time you reach for one that's ripe,
Watch out! You've started quite the hype.

A bonanza of giggles on this fine day,
Join the laughter, don't shy away.
These fruits of joy, so bright and bold,
Share secrets of wonder, always told.

The Lure of Sun-drenched Essence

Sunflowers whisper secrets untold,
While fruits bask in blankets of gold.
Their sweet aroma, a playful tease,
Invites all critters to come with ease.

Banana peels slide with cheeky glee,
While mischievous berries roll carefree.
Orange slices giggle, their zest in the air,
Making every moment a fruity affair.

A cantaloupe winks, a flirt on the vine,
Promising laughs in every lime.
With laughter and flavor, they create a scene,
Painting the day with a fruity sheen.

So gather the joy that nature imparts,
Join the dance from all of our hearts.
In this sunny patch, so wild and free,
The essence of fun is the key to glee!

Embracing the Gentle Drift

Tiny little creatures scurry about,
Wobbling on their feet, there's no doubt.
They laugh and tumble, roll down the hill,
Chasing after giggles that time can't still.

A dancer in a hat made of vine,
Whirls around, declares them divine.
With a swish and a flick, they aim for the sky,
Yet land in the mud, oh me, oh my!

A breeze sends them spinning, round and around,
Falling like confetti all over the ground.
They puff with laughter, at their great plight,
Who knew the fun could be such a sight?

In their merry chaos, joy's a sweet fable,
A slapstick saga, no need for a label.
With a sprinkle of humor, forever they play,
In the gentle drift, they brightened the day.

Radiant Gems Beneath the Canopy

Laughing ladies bask in the shade,
Giggling over plans that never quite made.
They wear crowns of leaves, not pearls but grass,
Their whispers of mischief? They'll never pass!

Plump little orbs hang low on the vine,
Popping with laughter, they're doing just fine.
Raucous games of tag in the afternoon light,
Dodging brisk breezes, they take off in flight.

Silly jests blossom ripe on the vine,
Who knew green thumbs could throw so much shine?
Beneath leafy shelters, they giggle and snack,
Sharing shrieks of joy as they bounce and hack.

Amidst radiant hues, a jamboree thrives,
Marvelous mayhem fuels their wild lives.
With nature's charm and chuckles galore,
Beneath the lush canopy, who could ask for more?

Palettes of a Blissful Harvest

Colors collide in a tangle of mess,
Brushing their cheeks as they laugh and confess.
Giggles erupt like fireworks in June,
Playtime and snacks make a splendid tune.

Splatters of joy paint the big ol' field,
From berry-finding quests; the fun is revealed.
Filling their baskets with wobbly things,
Adventures explode like a flock of bright wings.

Cartwheeling youngsters with arms wide and free,
Drenched in delight, oh where could they be?
A tumble here, a roll over there,
Sprinkled with laughter, they float like the air.

Beneath the warm sun, their shenanigans thrive,
Harvesting sweetness, they feel so alive.
With colors and chaos all over the scene,
A palette of giggles, a watery dream.

Mysteries of Twinkling Nightscapes

Under the moon, a riddle unfolds,
With whispers of secrets that nighttime holds.
They twirl in their pajamas, all carefree and bright,
Chasing the stars, giggles take flight.

They spot glowing orbs, thinking they must be,
The last of their toys lost by some greedy bee!
With sparkles and jokes exchanged on the ground,
Dancing through shadows, their laughter's profound.

In the cool evening breeze, a tickle like fun,
Their wild giggles fill the air, one by one.
Invisible crayons sketch the night sky,
Every sparkling star, a giggling reply.

Whimsical wonders wear costumes of dreams,
Their nights are alive with magical beams.
As mischief ignites in soft silver light,
The mysteries tumble, no end in sight!

www.ingramcontent.com/pod-product-compliance
Lightning Source LLC
Chambersburg PA
CBHW062108280426
43661CB00086B/326